SRA Reading Mastery
Signature Edition

Activities across the Curriculum
Grade 5

Siegfried Engelmann
Jean Osborn
Steve Osborn
Leslie Zoref

Mc Graw Hill **SRA**

Columbus, OH

SRAonline.com

Send all inquiries to this address:
SRA/McGraw-Hill
4400 Easton Commons
Columbus, OH 43219

ISBN: 978-0-07-612663-7
MHID: 0-07-612663-3

3 4 5 6 7 8 9 10 MAZ 13 12 11 10 09 08

The McGraw-Hill Companies

Table of Contents

Table of Contents - *Continued*

Table of Contents - *Continued*

What Is the Purpose of Activities across the Curriculum?

Reading Mastery Signature Edition, Grade 5, *Activities across the Curriculum* contains activities that you can use to reinforce and extend the concepts and skills your students are acquiring as they progress through *Reading Mastery.* The activities cover a range of content areas including science, social studies, geography, art, and language arts.

How Do I Use the Activities?

Activities across the Curriculum provides teacher directions for thirty-eight activities, some of which include blackline masters. Twenty-four blackline masters appear in the last part of this guide. The teacher directions for each activity specify the content area addressed, state the objective, and provide advice for evaluating student work.

Each activity is correlated to a specific lesson range in *Reading Mastery.* Lesson number references appear on each page of the directions. The activities come after every five lessons. You can present a given activity any time after the lesson specified in the directions. There are several activities for some lessons, while for others, there is only one activity.

Students do not have to do each activity. Rather, you should pick out the activities that will meet the needs and interests of your students. You can have the entire class work on a single activity or assign separate activities to groups of students. Some of the activities are for students to do on their own; other activities are to be done with a partner. Still other activities must be completed by small groups of students working together.

To use the activities:

- Select the activity that you wish to present and schedule it for a time after the students have completed their *Reading Mastery* lesson.

- Schedule sufficient time for the activity, but don't allow so much time that work on the activities seriously impedes your students' progress through *Reading Mastery.*

- Provide students with copies of blackline masters or other required materials.

- Check students' work by referring to the *Evaluation* segment in the teacher directions.

After Lesson 5

Math: Solving Problems

Objective: Students will solve problems about rate and time.

Directions: Tell students to read the directions and problems on Blackline Master 1. Ask them to use their math skills to solve the problems.

Evaluation:

1. 720

2. 600

3. 500

4. Theresa's

After Lesson 10

Geography: Then and Now

Objective: Students will compare a modern map with an ancient one.

Directions: Ask students to read the information and directions on Blackline Master 2. Then tell them to complete the activity independently. When students have finished, you may want to discuss some of the recent historical changes in Europe.

Evaluation: Students' maps should have current political boundaries drawn in. Countries, capitals, and major bodies of water should be labeled. Lists of corresponding locations should include the following:

Troy, in Turkey

Calypso, in Malta

Cyclops, Scylla, and cattle, in Sicily

Circe and Sirens, on islands off the western coast of Italy

Phacia and Ithaca, on islands off the western coast of Greece

ACTIVITY 3

After Lesson 15
Writing: Charting the Course of Odysseus

Objective: Students will complete a chart listing the places Odysseus has visited and the problems he has encountered.

Directions: Tell students to read the directions on Blackline Master 3. Then ask them to fill in the chart on their own. You may wish to have students work in pairs to complete the activity.

Evaluation: Students should list, in sequential order, the places Odysseus visited on his journey and the problems he encountered at each location.

ACTIVITY 4

After Lesson 20
Drama: Role-Playing

Objective: Students will perform a scene from "The Spider, the Cave, and the Pottery Bowl."

Directions: Divide the class into small groups. Ask each group to choose a scene from lessons 14 through 20 to act out. Allow time for each group to practice. Assign a time for each group to perform for the class.

Evaluation: Responses and interpretations will vary.

ACTIVITY 5

After Lesson 20
Art and Writing: Making a Clay Bowl

Objective: Students will organize and write the steps to take in making a clay bowl. Then they will draw a picture to illustrate at least one of the steps.

Directions: Have students read and complete Blackline Master 4. You may want to help them decide which step or steps to illustrate. After the projects are completed, ask students to read their explanations to the class.

Evaluation: Students' notes, explanations, and illustrations should correspond to the general directions in "The Spider, the Cave, and the Pottery Bowl."

ACTIVITY 6

After Lesson 25
Language and Writing: Using Vivid Language

Objective: Students will rewrite sentences, using more vivid language.

Directions: Have students read the information and directions on Blackline Master 5. You may want to write a few samples of vivid language on the board. Ask students for examples. Praise examples that are expressive and creative. Then have students complete the blackline master on their own.

When students have finished rewriting the sentences, have them work in pairs to read and evaluate each other's work.

Evaluation: Students' revisions will vary. Accept appropriate use of vivid language.

After Lesson 30

Social Studies and Geography: Where in the World Are You?

Objective: Students will locate Dublin, Ireland; New York City, New York; and their own city and state on a map. Then they will write a short paragraph telling how their ancestors reached the places where they settled.

Directions: Have students read the information and directions on Blackline Master 6. Then have them complete the project on their own. When students have completed their paragraphs, ask volunteers to read theirs to the class.

Evaluation: Responses will vary.

After Lesson 30

Language: Onomatopoeia

Objective: Students will understand onomatopoeia.

Directions: Explain to students that some words in the English language refer to sounds and sound like those sounds. Provide the following examples:

buzz   boom

hiss   thump

Have students write words for each of these sounds on a separate piece of paper:

1. a car's engine

2. a rainstorm

3. a horse running down a cobblestone road

4. a little puppy

5. an explosion

Evaluation: Responses will vary.

After Lesson 30

Art: Still Life

Objective: Students will draw or paint a still-life picture.

Directions: Explain to students that a still-life drawing is a drawing of an artistic arrangement of one or more objects (fruit, flowers, windows, books, or other objects). Remind students that the artist in "The Last Leaf" painted a still life on a brick wall.

Ask students to choose a medium that is comfortable for them and available to them (chalk, pencil, watercolor, crayon, or tempera). Then have them draw a still life of a plant, a handful of leaves, a vase of flowers, a bowl of fruit, a small pile of books, or any other ideas you have that are easy to assemble.

Evaluation: Students' artwork will vary. Encourage any creative, thoughtful expression.

After Lesson 35

Effective Speaking: Putting on a Skit

Objective: A group of students will put on a skit based on "Persephone."

Directions: Have students reread "Persephone" to determine the number of characters in the skit and what each character will do and say. Students may prepare a script, or they may speak from informal notes. Help them decide who will play each character. They may want to use some simple scenery to show where the story takes place. Give students time to practice their skit before they present it to the rest of the class. If the skit goes well, they can put it on for another classroom.

Evaluation: The skit should tell the story of "Persephone." Students should portray the characters in a convincing manner.

After Lesson 40
Writing: Poetry

Objective: Students will write a poem about a place.

Directions: Ask students to close their eyes and visualize Sara's attic room. Ask them to use their senses to perceive what the room is like. What does it smell like? What colors are in the room? Are there things that feel rough, soft, or smooth? What is the best place to sit or hide? What are the most interesting things to look at in the room?

Have the students write a short poem about the attic on a separate piece of paper. Direct them to write poems that appeal to the senses. Ask them to choose one or two senses to emphasize in their poems.

Evaluation: Students' poems will vary.

After Lesson 45
Science: Comparing and Contrasting Elements of Climate

Objective: Students will compare the climate of London, England, with their own climate.

Directions: Review with students what *climate* means. Tell them it is not just the weather in a certain location at a certain time, but weather that is typical for an area and can be expected year after year. Explain that climate refers to temperature and precipitation.

Ask students to read the information on Blackline Master 7. Then have them follow the directions on the blackline master and complete the assignment on their own.

Evaluation: Students' paragraphs should show similarities and differences between their own climate and London's climate.

ACTIVITY 13

After Lesson 50
Writing: Comparing a Book and a Movie

Objective: Students will determine differences between the novel *Sara Crewe* and a movie based on the book.

Directions: Arrange for your class to see the 1995 version of the movie *A Little Princess.* After they have watched the movie, have students read the directions on Blackline Master 8. Have them work in pairs to determine differences between the book and the movie. Then have them tell what they like best about the book and the movie.

Evaluation: Students should identify differences between the book and the movie. They should be able to describe differences in characters, setting, and plot. Students should also describe the parts they like best about the book and the movie.

ACTIVITY 14

After Lesson 55
Science: Air Pollution

Objective: Students will discuss causes of air pollution. Then they will write a paragraph about one reason for pollution and proposed solutions.

Directions: Lead a discussion about air pollution with students. Ask them to identify what they think causes pollution. Ask them whether burning leaves is good or bad for the environment (bad). Explain that when Robert McCloskey wrote "Mystery Yarn," people burned leaves everywhere in the United States and all over the world. Ask students how our awareness of air pollution has changed our lives in other ways.

After the discussion, have students choose one cause of pollution. Tell them to think about solutions for that type of pollution. Then have them write a paragraph about the problem and the proposed solutions. When students have finished writing, have them share their paragraphs with the rest of the class.

Evaluation: Students' paragraphs will vary. They should focus on one cause and should propose realistic solutions for that cause.

After Lesson 55

Math and Social Studies: Making a Bar Graph

Objective: Students will make a bar graph showing common household items that are recycled by their classmates.

Directions: Have students discuss their efforts to save and recycle things like plastic, paper clips, soft drink or aluminum cans, and so on. Ask them how reusing these items might help the environment (reduce waste, save natural resources).

Direct students to work in groups of six to list commonly-used household items that can be recycled. Then have students read the information and directions on Blackline Master 9 and complete the activity.

Evaluation: Students' bar graphs will vary. Students should discuss results of recycling items instead of throwing them away.

After Lesson 60

Science: Height of Trees

Objective: Students will read a diagram to compare the sizes of various trees.

Directions: Ask students to imagine climbing a tall tree, as Sylvia did in the story "A White Heron."

Have students read the information and directions on Blackline Master 10. Then have them answer the questions about the diagram.

Evaluation:

1. White ash

2. Douglas fir

3. 90 feet

4. 30 feet

5. Giant sequoia

After Lesson 65
Writing: An Interview with Jack London

Objective: Students will develop questions, conduct an interview, and write a news story about Jack London.

Directions: Have students reread lesson 61 in the textbook. Discuss questions students might ask Jack London. These should include questions about where he's from, where he lived, what he did, what he thought, and what he wrote. After students write down questions for the interview, break them into pairs. One student should conduct the interview while the other student pretends to be Jack London. After 5 to 10 minutes, have students switch places so each student gets a chance to conduct the interview. When both students have been interviewed, instruct them to write a news story about Jack London.

Evaluation: Students should develop questions that will help them write a news story about Jack London. Stories will vary but should reflect the information gathered from the "interview."

After Lesson 70
Writing: Developing Story Maps

Objective: Students will develop a story map for each of the first six chapters in *The Cruise of the Dazzler.*

Directions: Divide students into six groups. Then assign a different chapter from *The Cruise of the Dazzler* to each group. Have the students read the directions on Blackline Master 11. Then have them complete the story map for the chapter they were assigned. Have them refer to their textbooks to write the story maps. When they have completed the assignment, display the maps in sequence.

Evaluation: Students' story maps should reflect the content of each of the first six chapters of *The Cruise of the Dazzler.*

After Lesson 75

Writing: Developing Story Maps

Objective: Students will develop a story map for each of the last six chapters in *The Cruise of the Dazzler*.

Directions: Divide students into six groups. Then assign a different chapter from *The Cruise of the Dazzler* to each group. Have the students read the directions on Blackline Master 12. Then have them complete the story map for the chapter they were assigned. Have them refer to their textbooks to write the story maps. When they have completed the assignment, display the maps in sequence.

Evaluation: Students' story maps should reflect the content of each of the last six chapters of *The Cruise of the Dazzler*.

After Lesson 75

Writing: Comparing & Contrasting

Objective: Students will use Venn diagrams to help them write a description using comparison and contrast.

Directions: Explain to your class that Venn diagrams are made up of two or more overlapping circles. Venn diagrams are useful for examining similarities and differences in characters, stories, and poems. Have students read the directions and complete the Venn diagram on Blackline Master 13. Then, on a separate piece of paper, have them write a short description of each boy.

Evaluation: Students' Venn diagrams should include similarities and differences between Joe and Frisco Kid. Their descriptions should highlight the information on their Venn diagrams.

After Lesson 75

Music: Composing Lyrics

Objective: Students will write lyrics to a song about baseball.

Directions: Tell students about the song "Take Me Out to the Ball Game." If possible, play it for them. Then divide them into small groups and have them write a song about baseball. The song can be about anything related to baseball—real or imaginary. Encourage students to be creative. When they have finished writing their song, have each group perform it for the rest of the class.

Evaluation: Songs should reflect students' knowledge of baseball.

After Lesson 80

Social Studies: A Nation Divided

Objective: Students will understand that the states were divided over their views on slavery. They will also understand that slavery was a key issue leading to the Civil War.

Directions: Have students read the information and directions on Blackline Master 14. Then have them complete the activity.

Evaluation:

1. 24

2. 16; Virginia, North Carolina, South Carolina, Georgia, Florida, Alabama, Mississippi, Louisiana, Texas, Arkansas, Tennessee, Missouri, Kentucky, Maryland, Delaware, West Virginia

3. 19; Maine, New Hampshire, Vermont, Connecticut, Massachusetts, Rhode Island, New Jersey, New York, Pennsylvania, Ohio, Indiana, Illinois, Michigan, Wisconsin, Iowa, Minnesota, Kansas, Oregon, California

4. Missouri, Kentucky, West Virginia, Maryland, Delaware

5. The Confederacy

After Lesson 80

Social Studies and Geography: Tracing the Underground Railroad

Objective: Using a map, students will trace stops along the Underground Railroad. Then they will explain how the operation worked.

Directions: Discuss where Harriet Tubman was from and how she and others ran the Underground Railroad. Then ask students to read the information and directions on Blackline Master 15. Suggest that they use an encyclopedia or the Internet to learn more about Harriet Tubman and the Underground Railroad.

Evaluation: Students' maps should reflect information provided in the text. Their paragraphs should explain how the Underground Railroad worked. They should also tell that it was successful because of courageous people like Harriet Tubman and helpful whites who were against slavery.

After Lesson 80

Writing: Writing a Letter

Objective: Students will write a letter from a formerly enslaved person who escaped to freedom on the Underground Railroad.

Directions: Have students try to imagine what it must have been like for a person like Jim to arrive in Canada. Ask students to pretend they have just arrived in Canada using the Underground Railroad. Have each student write a letter to a family member on a separate piece of paper. Each student should tell about the adventures on the Underground Railroad and how he or she feels about finally being free.

Evaluation: Students' letters should follow acceptable letter format. They should relate their adventures on the journey to freedom. Their letters should also convey how students feel about freedom.

After Lesson 85
Art: Recruitment Poster

Objective: Students will make a Civil War recruitment poster directed at formerly enslaved persons.

Directions: Have students design a recruitment poster for the Civil War directed at formerly enslaved persons. Explain that the Union Army encouraged formerly enslaved persons to sign up to fight in restricted regiments.

Have students research the Civil War so their posters reflect the era. They may need to consult a social studies textbook or other classroom reference materials to complete this project. Please guide them to appropriate resources.

Evaluation: Posters will vary.

After Lesson 85
Drama and Writing: Writing Dialogue

Objective: Students will practice writing dialogue.

Directions: Have students reread the play *All in Favor.* Explain to them what dialogue is. Then divide the class into pairs and have them write an additional scene at the end of the play. In this scene, Harriet and Sidney return to the clubhouse to find Nancy, Eddie, Dorothy, and Alvin holding their first club meeting. Have them write the new scene in the same format as the rest of the play.

Evaluation: Students' dialogues should follow the format in the text. Content will vary.

ACTIVITY 27

After Lesson 90

Poetry and Language: Choral Reading

Objective: Students will read "Miracles" as a choral reading.

Directions: Assign students specific lines to read from the poem "Miracles" by Walt Whitman. Then direct them to read their lines aloud in turn. Have students practice phrasing and coordination with other students in the class. After a few practices, they can perform their choral reading for another class.

Evaluation: Students should read as one voice.

ACTIVITY 28

After Lesson 90

Social Studies: Description of a River Town in the 1840s

Objective: Students will write a description of a typical river town in the 1840s.

Directions: Have students reread "Life in the 1840s" in their textbook. Then have them complete Blackline Master 16. If needed, direct them to the school library or the Internet to get additional information about river towns in the 1840s.

Evaluation: Charts should parallel material presented in the text.

After Lesson 95

Math: Story Problems

Objective: Students will calculate answers to story problems.

Directions: Have students read the directions on Blackline Master 17. Then have them complete the problems on their own. When they are finished, go over the answers with them.

Evaluation:

1. 25 cents

2. 3 hours; 30 cents

3. 5-½ hours

4. 44 buckets

5. 132 boards

After Lesson 95

Writing: Writing to Persuade

Objective: Students will write a short persuasive composition.

Directions: Have students think of something they had to do but didn't want to—like whitewash a fence. Tell them to read the information and directions on Blackline Master 18. Then have them write their persuasive composition on a separate piece of paper.

Evaluation: Students' compositions should vary but should incorporate their pre-writing notes.

After Lesson 100
Art and Drama: Advertising

Objective: Students will design a poster to promote a play based on a scene in *Tom Sawyer.*

Directions: Ask students to choose one of the first ten chapters of *Tom Sawyer* and to design a poster promoting a play based on the chapter. Tell them the poster should answer the following questions:

• What is the title of the play?

• What kind of play is it (drama, comedy, musical)?

• Who are the characters?

• Where will the play be performed?

• When will the play be performed?

Tell students to illustrate their posters with pictures of the characters or a vivid scene from the play. Remind them to include words or phrases that will attract an audience.

Evaluation: Students' dialogues and promotional material will vary but should reflect their understanding of the characters and the scene taken from the story.

After Lesson 100
Writing: Developing Story Maps

Objective: Students will develop a story map for chapters 1 through 10 of *Tom Sawyer.*

Directions: Divide students into ten groups. Assign one chapter to each group. Ask students to read the directions on Blackline Master 19. Tell them to complete the story map for the chapter they were assigned. Remind them to refer to their textbooks to complete their story maps. After they've finished the assignment, display the story maps in sequence.

Evaluation: Students' story maps should reflect the content of the assigned chapters of *Tom Sawyer.*

After Lesson 105
Social Studies and Geography: The Importance of Rivers and Trails in the Mid-1800s

Objective: Students will understand the importance of the Mississippi River, other rivers, and trails during the mid-1800s in the United States.

Directions: Have students read the information and directions on Blackline Master 20. Then have them complete the project.

Evaluation:

1. Ohio River

2. Oregon Trail, California Trail

3. Mississippi River, Missouri River

4. Old Spanish Trail

5. St. Louis, Memphis, Natchez, New Orleans

ACTIVITY 34

After Lesson 110
Writing: Developing Story Maps

Objective: Students will develop a story map for chapters 11 through 20 of *Tom Sawyer.*

Directions: Divide students into ten groups. Assign one chapter to each group. Ask students to read the directions on Blackline Master 21. Tell them to complete the story map for the chapter they were assigned. Remind them to refer to their textbooks to complete their story maps. After they've finished the assignment, display the story maps in sequence.

Evaluation: Students' story maps should reflect the content of the assigned chapters of *Tom Sawyer.*

After Lesson 110

Drama: A Mock Trial

Objective: Students will participate in a trial based on the one in chapter 16 of *Tom Sawyer.*

Directions: Have students reread lesson 106 in the textbook. Assign students to play the judge, two lawyers, Muff Potter, witnesses, and a jury. Allow time for the lawyers to prepare their cases. Then conduct the trial. Encourage students to exercise their imaginations without deviating from the facts in the text.

Evaluation: The mock trial should reflect the facts as presented in chapter 16 of *Tom Sawyer.*

After Lesson 115

Science: Caves—Stalactites and Stalagmites

Objective: Students will use information to write a paragraph about stalactites and stalagmites.

Directions: Have students read the information and directions on Blackline Master 22. Then have them write their paragraphs on a separate piece of paper.

Evaluation: Students' paragraphs should summarize the basic definitions of the two formations.

After Lesson 120

Writing: Developing Story Maps

Objective: Students will develop a story map for chapters 21 through 30 of *Tom Sawyer.*

Directions: Divide students into ten groups. Assign one chapter to each group. Ask students to read the directions on Blackline Master 23. Tell them to complete the story map for the chapter they were assigned. Remind them to refer to their textbooks to complete their story maps. After they've finished the assignment, display the story maps in sequence.

Evaluation: Students' story maps should reflect the content of the assigned chapters of *Tom Sawyer.*

After Lesson 120

Writing: Comparing and Contrasting Characters

Objective: Students will develop lists of characteristics for Tom Sawyer, Huck Finn, and Becky Thatcher about their family situations, attitudes toward family life, and their goals. Then students will write an essay comparing and contrasting the characters based on the information in the lists.

Directions: Have students read the directions on Blackline Master 24. Then have them complete the chart. When they have finished, have them write an essay that compares and contrasts the three characters' family situations.

Evaluation: Students should list the characters' family relationships, feelings, and goals. Their essays should reflect details listed in their charts.

ACTIVITY 1: Solving Problems

Directions: Use your math skills to solve each problem below. Write your answers on the blanks.

1. If a doughnut machine makes 12 doughnuts in one minute, how many doughnuts can it make in one hour? (There are 60 minutes in an hour.)

   _____

2. If the O-So-Lite doughnut machine can make 50 doughnuts an hour, how many doughnuts can it make in 12 hours?

   _____

3. Johnson's Doughnut Stand sold 144 doughnuts on Monday, 66 doughnuts on Tuesday, 101 doughnuts on Wednesday, 84 doughnuts on Thursday, and 105 doughnuts on Friday. How many doughnuts were sold during the week?

   _____

4. There are two coffee shops in Duncan City. Oscar's shop sells a large cup of coffee and a doughnut for $1.55; a cup of coffee by itself is $.75, and a doughnut by itself is $.90. Theresa's shop sells a small cup of coffee for $.55 and a large cup of coffee for $.75; all doughnuts cost $.85 each. Both shops sell milk for $.50 a carton.
   The Vine family wants to buy one large coffee, three doughnuts, and two cartons of milk. At which shop will they get a lower price?

   _____

Directions: Compare the maps below. Some of the present-day countries you have read about or heard about are not on the large map that shows the region of Odysseus's voyages. On the large map, draw in boundaries for the countries that now make up this region. Write the current names of the countries and their capitals. Label the main bodies of water. Then make a list of the people and places Odysseus visited on his journey home, beginning with Troy. Tell where these places are located on the present-day map.

Odysseus's Voyage Then

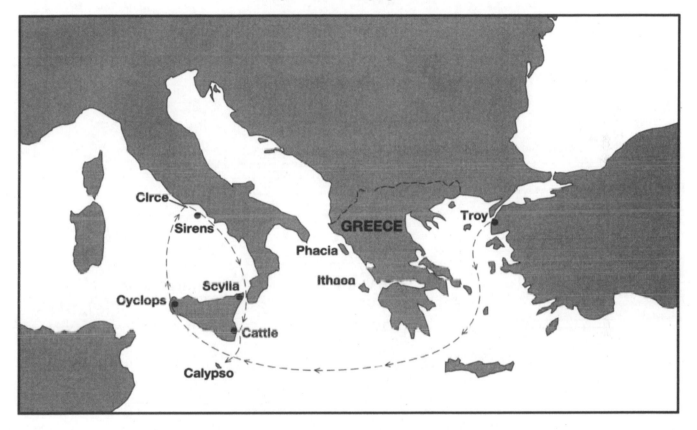

Present-Day

Charting the Course of Odysseus

Directions: By the time Odysseus reaches Phacia, he has had many adventures and traveled many miles. Trace his steps since he left Troy. Next to each leg of his trip, write the problems he faced.

The Travels of Odysseus

He left Troy   **and went to**   **Problems**

_____ _____

_____

_____

He left   **and went to**   **Problems**

_____ _____

_____

_____

He left   **and went to**   **Problems**

_____ _____

_____

_____

He left   **and went to**   **Problems**

_____ _____

_____

_____

Finally Odysseus reaches Phacia.

ACTIVITY 5: Making a Clay Bowl

Directions: Kate didn't know much about making a clay bowl at first, but she was able to follow her grandmother's instructions. Reread lesson 20 to review the steps Kate took in making the bowl. Use the categories below to write out the steps in detail. When you have finished listing the steps, use your notes to write a few paragraphs on a separate piece of paper explaining how to make a clay bowl. Include one or more illustrations of the steps in the process.

Before making the bowl

_____

_____

_____

Starting to make the bowl

_____

_____

_____

Finishing the bowl

_____

_____

_____

Baking the bowl

_____

_____

_____

ACTIVITY 6: Using Vivid Language

Directions: Look at the following sentences. One of them uses vivid language to describe what Johnny is doing. Which sentence is more interesting to read?

Johnny looked at the baseball.

Johnny's brown eyes grew larger as he stared at the baseball.

The second sentence uses vivid language. It is more interesting to read than the first sentence. In your writing, use colorful language to show your readers what is happening. Rewrite each sentence below, using vivid language.

1. The goat had to eat.

   _____

2. The next day the second son fed the goat.

   _____

3. The tailor went to the stall.

   _____

4. He took the goat to the pasture.

   _____

5. His master gave him a table.

   _____

6. The innkeeper remembered he had a table like it.

   _____

7. The young man went to the stable and shut the door.

   _____

8. The old tailor could not believe such a thing.

   _____

     Blackline Master 5

ACTIVITY 7:   Where in the World Are You?

Directions: Look at the map below. Locate Dublin, Ireland. Then locate New York City in New York. Draw a line between the two.

The Dunn family discovered there were people in New York City who had come from other places or who represented other cultures. Locate where you live on the map and draw a line to the area your ancestors came from. That place may lie in Europe, Africa, Asia, or other parts of the Americas, including the United States. If you are not sure, talk to adults in your family who may know.

Write a paragraph telling how your ancestors may have reached the place where they settled.

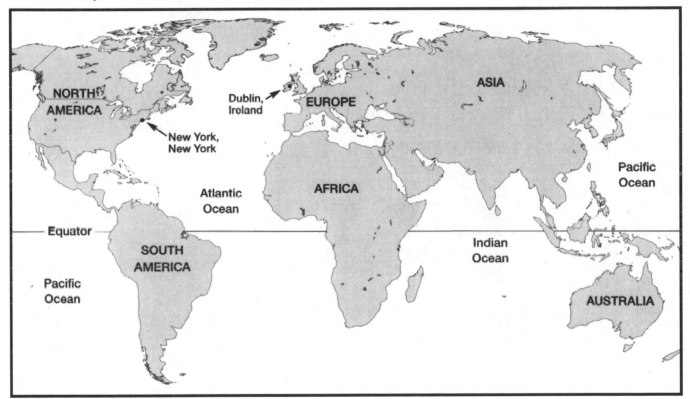

Comparing and Contrasting Elements of Climate

Directions: Look at the climate map below. Compare the climate of London with the climate in the area where you live. Then look at the weather for London. Compare the weather in London with the weather where you live. Use the chart below to make notes. Then, on a separate piece of paper, write a paragraph that compares and contrasts the two climates. Tell about similarities and differences in spring, summer, fall, and winter.

Average Monthly Weather

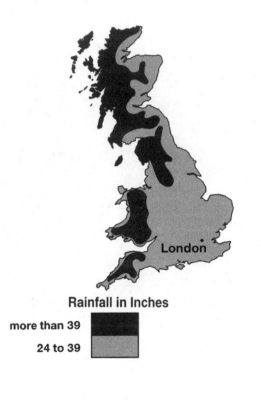

Rainfall in Inches

more than 39

24 to 39

	London Temperatures				Days of rain or snow
	F°		C°		
	High	Low	High	Low	
Jan.	44	35	7	2	17
Feb.	45	35	7	2	13
Mar.	51	37	11	3	11
Apr.	56	40	13	4	14
May	63	45	17	7	13
June	69	51	21	11	11
July	73	55	23	13	13
Aug.	72	54	22	12	13
Sept.	67	51	19	11	13
Oct.	58	44	14	7	14
Nov.	49	39	9	4	16
Dec.	45	36	7	2	16

Seasons	Our Climate	London's Climate
Spring		
Summer		
Fall		
Winter		

ACTIVITY 13: Comparing a Book and a Movie

Directions: With a partner, make a list of the ways the book and the movie you saw are different. Tell what is different about the characters, setting, and plot. Then list what you liked best in the book and what you liked best in the movie.

	Sara Crewe	*A Little Princess*
Characters		
Setting		
Plot		
What I Liked Best		

ACTIVITY 15: Making a Bar Graph

Directions: Make a list of five common household items that can be recycled. Write each item on lines at the bottom of the chart. Ask the members of your group which of those items they recycle. Create a **bar graph** of your results by coloring in the number of boxes above each item that represents the number of students who recycle that item.

When all the graphs are complete, compare your results with those of the other groups. What conclusions can you draw from the results?

Number of Students Who Recycle

	Item 1	Item 2	Item 3	Item 4	Item 5
6					
5					
4					
3					
2					
1					
Name of Item	Item 1 _____	Item 2 _____	Item 3 _____	Item 4 _____	Item 5 _____

ACTIVITY 16: Height of Trees

Directions: The diagram below compares the heights of different trees found in different regions of the United States. Use the diagram to answer the questions.

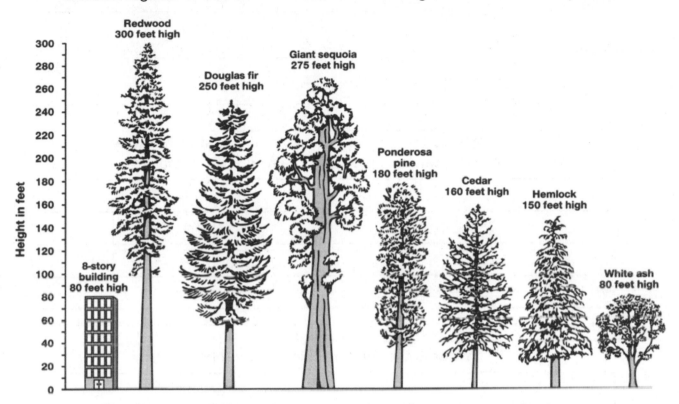

1. Which tree is the same height as an 8-story building?

   _____

2. Which tree would be as tall as a 25-story building?

   _____

3. How much taller is the Douglas fir than the cedar?

   _____

4. How much shorter is the hemlock than the ponderosa pine?

   _____

5. Which tree is taller than the Douglas fir but shorter than the redwood?

   _____

ACTIVITY 18: Developing Story Maps

Directions: Use this story map to summarize your chapter from *The Cruise of the Dazzler*.

Title _____

Author _____

Chapter _____

Settings (Where does the chapter take place?)	Main Characters (Who are the main characters?)

Problem
(What is the main problem in the chapter?)

Events
(What are the main events in this chapter?)

Outcome
(What happens at the end of the chapter?)

Blackline Master 11

Directions: Use this story map to summarize your chapter from *The Cruise of the Dazzler.*

Title _____

Author _____

Chapter _____

Settings (Where does the chapter take place?)	Main Characters (Who are the main characters?)

Problem
(What is the main problem in the chapter?)

Events
(What are the main events in this chapter?)

Outcome
(What happens at the end of the chapter?)

Directions: In each circle below, list the different characteristics of Joe and Frisco Kid. In the space where the circles overlap, list the characteristics that the two boys have in common. Then, on a separate piece of paper, write a short description of each boy.

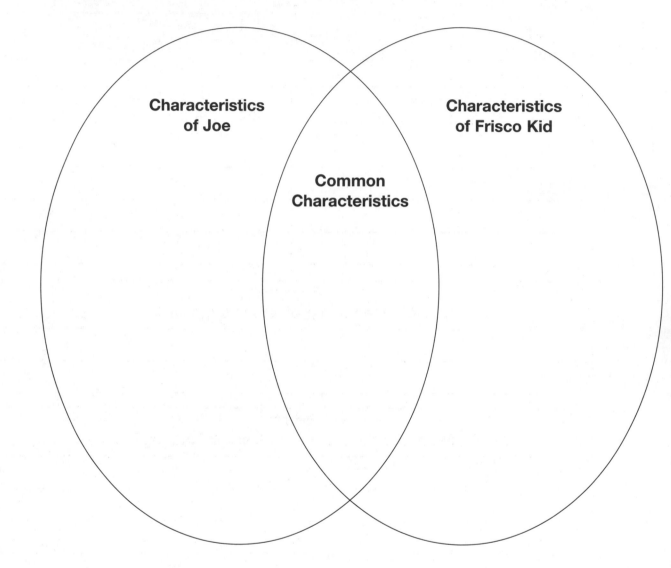

Characteristics of Joe

Characteristics of Frisco Kid

Common Characteristics

ACTIVITY 22:   A Nation Divided

Directions: Before the Civil War, slavery was against the law in more than half the states. Some states in which slavery was still legal *seceded,* or withdrew, from the Union in 1861. Other slave states did not secede.

Study the map below and answer the questions that follow.

The United States in 1861

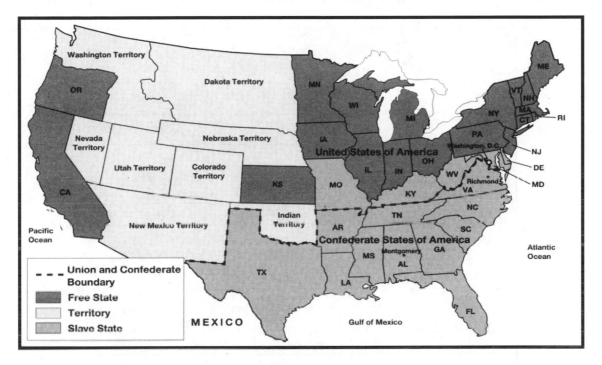

1. How many states were in the Union in 1861?

   _____

2. In how many states was slavery legal? Name those states.

   _____

3. In how many states was slavery illegal? Name those states.

   _____

4. Five "border" states were uncertain about whether they should secede or stay in the Union. Which states were the "border" states?

   _____

5. What were the states that seceded from the Union in 1861 called?

Directions: Think about what you have read about Harriet Tubman and the Underground Railroad. Use an encyclopedia or the Internet to learn more. Look at the map below. Draw a line showing the route of the "railroad."

When you have completed the map, use the space below to write a paragraph explaining how the Underground Railroad operated. Then tell why it was successful.

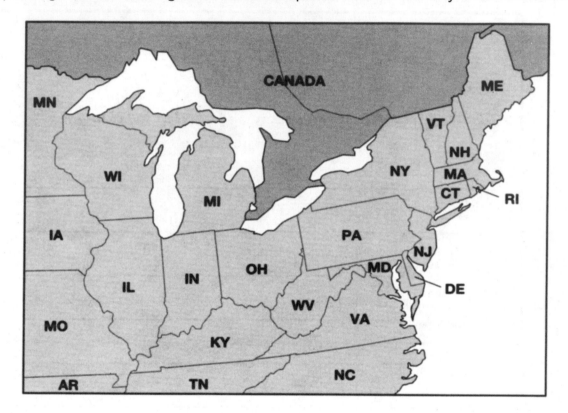

_____

_____

_____

_____

_____

_____

_____

ACTIVITY 28: Description of a River Town in the 1840s

Directions: Use the information in the text to help you plan, write, and draw a description of a river town in the 1840s. Visit your library or the Internet to learn more. Use the chart below to help you plan your city.

Life on the Mississippi

Name of town:	
Population:	
Features of the town:	
School life:	
Home life:	
Transportation:	
Other:	

ACTIVITY 29:   Story Problems

Directions: Use the information below to answer the following questions.

Tom Sawyer had to whitewash his aunt Polly's fence. Because he wanted to finish early to go fishing, he decided to pay his friends to help him. He offered them ten cents an hour to paint the fence.

1. Becky Thatcher helped Tom whitewash the fence for two and a half hours. How much money did she make?

   _____

2. Tom's brother Sid worked from 8:00 a.m. to 9:30 a.m. Then he worked from 10:00 a.m. to 11:30 a.m. How many hours did he work? How much money did he make?

   _____

3. If Billy Fisher wanted to make fifty-five cents, how many hours would he have to work?

   _____

Aunt Polly's fence is 132 feet long. Tom figured that it would take one bucket of whitewash for every three boards in the fence. Each board in the fence is one foot wide.

4. How many buckets of whitewash are needed to finish the fence?

   _____

5. How many boards are in Aunt Polly's fence?

   _____

ACTIVITY 30: Writing to Persuade

Directions: Think about how Tom Sawyer convinced his friends to whitewash his aunt Polly's fence. Now think about something you don't like to do. You are going to write a short passage that should persuade someone to do the unpleasant task in your place. Use the space below to organize your writing. Then write your composition on a separate piece of paper.

Task you don't want to do: _____

What reasons will you give to convince someone to do it for you? Give three reasons.

Reason 1:

_____

_____

_____

Reason 2:

_____

_____

_____

Reason 3:

_____

_____

_____

Summary:

_____

_____

_____

ACTIVITY 32: Developing Story Maps

Directions: Use this story map to summarize your chapter from *Tom Sawyer*.

Title _____

Author _____

Chapter _____

Settings (Where does the chapter take place?)	Main Characters (Who are the main characters?)

Problem (What is the main problem in the chapter?)

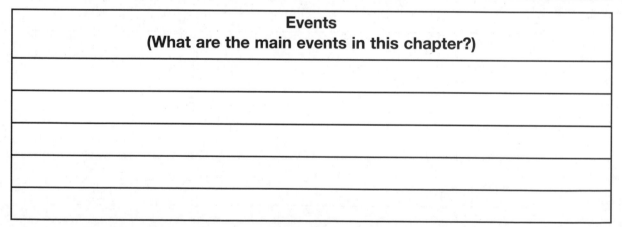

Events (What are the main events in this chapter?)

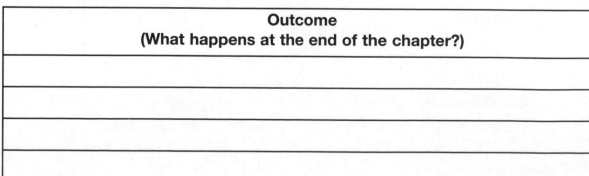

Outcome (What happens at the end of the chapter?)

ACTIVITY 33: The Importance of Rivers and Trails in the Mid-1800s

Directions: Look at the map below. It shows the Mississippi River and other major rivers and trails in the United States. During the mid-1800s, rivers were important in transporting goods and people across the nation. Trails were also well-traveled routes that helped people find the best way to get from one place to another. Study the map. Then use it to answer the questions that follow.

1. What body of water would you use to travel from Pittsburgh to Louisville?

   _____

2. What trails would you use if you were traveling from Independence to Sacramento?

   _____

3. On what two rivers is St. Louis located?

   _____

4. What trail links Santa Fe to Los Angeles?

   _____

5. Name the cities on this map that are on the Mississippi River.

   _____

   _____

ACTIVITY 34: Developing Story Maps

Directions: Use this story map to summarize your chapter from *Tom Sawyer*.

Title _____

Author _____

Chapter _____

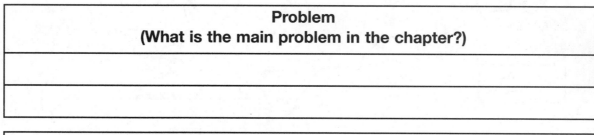

Settings (Where does the chapter take place?)	Main Characters (Who are the main characters?)

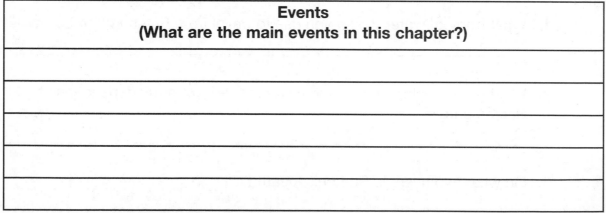

Problem (What is the main problem in the chapter?)

Events (What are the main events in this chapter?)

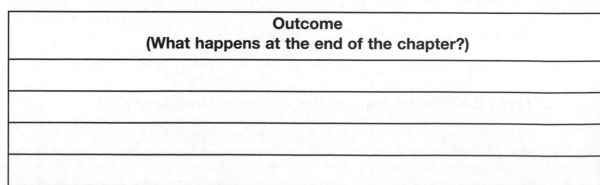

Outcome (What happens at the end of the chapter?)

ACTIVITY 36: Caves—Stalactites and Stalagmites

Directions: Natural caves are hollow chambers in the earth. Read the following information about caves.

Stalactites and stalagmites are spectacular natural formations found in limestone caves. Stalactites hang from the ceiling, while stalagmites build up from the floor of the cave.

Stalactites and stalagmites are created by underground water flow. The water trickles down through cracks in limestone caves. The water slowly dissolves the mineral calcite, which is in the limestone. Because the water cannot carry all the calcite, small amounts of calcite deposit on the cave ceiling. This process is repeated for each drop of water that trickles down. After many years, stalactites made of calcite form like icicles from the cave ceiling. When the water drips, it also forms the cone-shaped stalagmites that build up from the cave floor. Stalactites and stalagmites are often found in pairs, joining in the center to form pillars or columns.

Write a paragraph about stalactites and stalagmites. Be sure to explain what they are and how they are formed. Include their similarities and differences. Use the space below to write a rough draft. Then on a separate piece of paper, write your final draft. You may wish to include an illustration with your paragraph.

_____

_____

_____

_____

_____

_____

_____

_____

Developing Story Maps

Directions: Use this story map to summarize your chapter from *Tom Sawyer*.

Title _____

Author _____

Chapter _____

Settings (Where does the chapter take place?)	Main Characters (Who are the main characters?)

Problem (What is the main problem in the chapter?)

Events (What are the main events in this chapter?)

Outcome (What happens at the end of the chapter?)

Comparing and Contrasting Characters

Directions: Think of what you know about Tom Sawyer, Huck Finn, Becky Thatcher, and their family situations. First, complete the chart. Then use the information to write a composition using comparison and contrast on a separate piece of paper.

Characters	What is the character's family situation?	How does the character feel about family?	What are the character's goals?
Tom			
Huck			
Becky			